Someone
AWESOME

May you be able to know, with all God's children, God's love.
May you know how long, how wide, how deep, and how high his love is.
May you taste it for yourselves.
It is so great you will never see the end of it.
You won't fully know or understand it.
But at last you will be filled up with God himself.

EPHESIANS 3:18-19, SLB

To the faithful Bible teachers
at River Road Baptist Church
in Eugene, Oregon
from 1954 to 1974.
I really WAS listening!

Someone
AWESOME

By Larry Libby • Illustrations by Tim Jonke

Gold 'n'
Honey
BOOKS

"Special Edition, printed for
Reading's Fun, Ltd."

SOMEONE AWESOME

published by Gold 'n' Honey Books
a part of the Questar publishing family

© 1995 by Questar Publishers, Inc.
Designed by David Carlson and David Uttley

International Standard Book Number: 0-88070-632-5

Printed in Spain

For information:
Questar Publishers, Inc.
Post Office Box 1720
Sisters, Oregon 97759

96 97 98 99 00 01 02 -- 10 9 8 7 6 5 4 3 2

Someone Awesome

Imagine you made up a word.

A special word.

A most amazing word.

The best word you ever thought or said.

No one in the whole wide world has ever used that word.

No one has ever heard it,

    no one has ever said it,

        no one has ever sung it,

            no one has even thought it,

because it is *your* word. (And if some Eskimo in his igloo a hundred years ago accidentally mumbled the word in his sleep, that wouldn't really count, because he'd never remember it.)

Now, it's kind of a rule that words have to *mean* something. I don't know who made up that rule, but that's the way it seems to be. So let's say that you have given this word of yours the BEST meaning you could. And every time you say this word to yourself, it reminds you of things more wonderful than you could tell in any plain, used-up kind of words.

It's like Christmas—and your birthday—and fishing with your Grampa—and hearing your favorite song—and Disneyland—and hitting a home run—and laughing with your best friend—and finding your lost dog…all wrapped up in one word. (But it's a lot more than that, too.)

Now let's say something happens to your word. Something terrible.

You write your word down on a piece of paper (a huge mistake) and leave it lying on your dresser (an even huger mistake). And that pesky little neighbor kid who always snoops around your room and gets into your stuff picks up that piece of paper and *learns your word.*

What that kid does with your word—your Very Own Word— is as horrible as you might imagine. Right away he starts blabbing it all over the place like it's a big joke, and teasing you with it, and singing it in dumb little songs that sound like television commercials.

Before long, the whole neighborhood knows your word, and all the kids at school. Everybody starts saying it and writing it in notes and joking around with it and someone even uses it to name his pet goldfish.

What would have happened to your word?

Would it still be special?

Would it still say all you wanted it to say?

Would it still mean all you wanted it to mean?

What would happen when you tried to *use* your Very Own Word to tell somebody something important? Instead of seeing how amazing and important your word was, she might shrug her shoulders and say, "Oh, *that*."

That's a little like how I feel about saying, "God is awesome."

"Sure," someone says, "and I had an awesome hamburger for lunch, wore my awesome sneakers to school, and played an awesome video game at the mall yesterday."

See what I mean? How do you say, "I had an awesome hamburger," and then turn around and say, "*God* is Someone Awesome"?

Awesome really means "full of awe." And A-W-E is something you feel deep in your chest when you see something or someone

> bigger
>> brighter
>>> greater
>>>> deeper
>>>>> higher
>>>>>> stronger
>>>>>>> finer

than anything or anyone you've ever seen before.

"Awesome" used to be such a strong word that there was really only one person anywhere you could say it about.

And it wasn't a king or queen or general or president or ball player or any other important, flashy person.

It was God.

God is awesome.

The Bible calls him *"The great, mighty and awesome God"* (*Nehemiah 9:32, NIV*).

If you could ever see Him, the way He REALLY IS, your eyes would get wide as sand dollars. Your knees would feel weak and trembly. Your mouth would drop open. Your voice (if you could say anything at all) would creak like an old door. Your heart would thud so hard it might bruise your ribs.

And you would probably end up flat on your face before Him.

Why? Because HE IS AWESOME.

He is awesome like nothing or nobody else. Anywhere. Ever.

That's why you and I have so many questions about God. That's why we have such a hard time understanding things about Him sometimes. That's why we'll *never* have all the answers we want, even when we want those answers so very much.

But I still think it's good to ask questions, don't you? I still think we ought to ask and ask and ask...even if people who write books don't always have such good answers.

So let's go right ahead and do that! Let's ask some questions and then think about answers together.

Maybe we'll find out that "awesome" can never be a something at all.

Only a SOMEONE.

And a Someone who loves us very much.

IF GOD MADE EVERYTHING,
THEN WHO MADE GOD?

*N*ow that's a very hard question for a first question. The answer is that *no one* made God. If someone *had* made God, that someone would have to be greater and wiser and stronger than God.

But no one is. No one could ever be.

God, you see, was never "made" at all. Never created. Never born.

He always was. He always will be.

But…how could THAT be?

Do you have a little brother or sister? Can you remember the day the baby was born? Can you remember the day Mom brought that tiny bundle home from the hospital? Here was a brand new little person, all wrapped in pink or blue. And it's kind of funny to think that before that baby began to be, he or she just wasn't!

Maybe you've seen pictures of yourself way back when you were a baby. It's a little strange to think that before you began life inside your mom, there was no *you*!

You weren't here. You weren't there. You weren't anywhere at all. You just *weren't*, and that's all there is to it. No one could even imagine "you" because there was nothing to imagine.

But then—in a moment—in a miracle—YOU began!

And after you were born and joined your family, it was hard to think of a time when there wasn't a you. (And I'm so glad there is a you, after all. It's so much nicer having you here.)

But God never began anywhere. There never was a time when God *wasn't*. He's always been.

Before you were born…

Before your mom and dad were born…

Before your great, great, ever-so-great grandparents were born…

Before anyone on the whole world was born…

Before there even was a world…

Before the planets or moons or stars or angels…

Before anything that ever was…

Before, before, before, before.

Before there was light or dark.

Before there was hot or cold.

Before there was up or down.

Before there was far or near.

Before there was here or there.

Before anything at all, *God* was…just the same as He is now…a wonderful, loving, wise, powerful God.

Of course it has to be that way, because *someone* had to create everything. And that someone has to be the greatest someone of all. There was no one before God, and there is no one greater than He.

In the last book of the Bible, the Lord says,

"I am the A and the Z. I am the Beginning and the End. I am the First and Last" (Revelation 22:13, SLB).

When someone says, "I am the A and the Z," that pretty much covers everything, doesn't it? That means His life goes farther back than you could ever think and farther ahead than you could ever imagine—no matter how good your imagination is.

So where did God *come from*?

He didn't come from anywhere, because He was always everywhere.

Now these sorts of questions can make your mind swirl round and round, and these sorts of answers might not be the kind you really want at all. But listen—there's even a reason for that!

⌐When we find ourselves so very puzzled about God, when we've stretched our poor brains as far as we can stretch them and we *still* can't understand, that helps us remember that God is bigger than our minds. He's bigger and stronger and higher and finer than our best thoughts about Him. *No one* can begin to understand everything about Him! Even the apostle Paul, good and wise as he was, could only shake his head and say,

"Oh, what a wonderful God we have! How great are his wisdom and knowledge and riches! We can't know his decisions and his methods! For who among us can know the mind of the Lord?…For everything comes from God alone. Everything lives by his power. Everything is for his glory. To him be glory ever more!" (Romans 11:33, 34, 36, SLB)

What God *does* tell us, in the very first words of the Bible, is that He was there "In the beginning." When everything got started, God was right there, making it all happen just the way He wanted it to happen. And maybe that's all we really need to know.

Just imagine this. Early one morning you open your eyes, and your room is filled with morning light, soft as a robin's feather, yellow and mellow as butter. It's cozy and warm under your quilts, and you can smell pancakes and sweet bacon sizzling in the kitchen. And the first thing you notice as your eyes get used to the light is your mom sitting there in her bathrobe beside your bed. She's looking down at you, with so much love in her eyes.

Now (if you felt like it) you could ask her a lot of questions. You could say, "What's going on? Why are you here? How long have you been sitting there? How did you know when I was going to wake up? Why do you love me so much?"

Or…instead of worrying over all those questions…you could just wrap your arms around her neck, give her a big hug, and tumble out of bed in the fresh sunlight for a cup of hot chocolate and a steaming plate of pancakes and maple syrup.

God wants us to believe Him and love Him and obey Him and *enjoy* Him, even though we don't understand everything about Him. He wants us to open our eyes every morning with thanks and gladness bubbling up in our hearts that such a big, powerful God loves us very, very much and fills our lives with good things.

He'll be there for us. Every morning. Every night. Just like always.

And always and always and always.

WHAT DOES GOD LOOK LIKE?

When I was very little, I thought I knew just what God looked like. Whenever I closed my eyes and thought about God, I pictured Mrs. Eickmeyer.

Now I know that God is God, and that He isn't a lady (or a man, either), but still…every time I thought about Heaven and God up there on His throne and angels flying around, I saw the calm, smiling face of Mrs. Eickmeyer right in the middle of it all.

Mrs. Eickmeyer was the nice lady who worked in the church nursery when I was little. And whenever my parents went into big-people church, they would first take me downstairs, kiss me, hand me to Mrs. Eickmeyer, and tell me to learn all I could about *God*. How was I supposed to know that God wasn't Mrs. Eickmeyer? I probably thought they were handing me off to God!

I liked Mrs. Eickmeyer very much. She had a big, white, wooden box full of toys, told me stories about Jesus in a high, soft voice, and gave me graham crackers. We had a great time. Honest, I can still remember it.

The only problem was, for years and years after that (and even though I knew better), I always thought about God looking just like her: that smiling lady in the gray silky blouse, with the round, wire-frame glasses and her hair tied up in a bun.

Now the truth is, God the Father is a spirit, and He is *invisible*. The Bible says He is *"the King of all kings and the Lord of all lords. He is the only One who never dies. He lives in light so bright no one can go near it. No one has ever seen God, or can see him"* (1 Timothy 6:15-16).

God lives in an ocean of blinding light—brighter than the burning heart of a great star. No human being has ever seen Him.

That was something that really bothered one friend of Jesus named Philip.

All twelve of the Lord's followers were together with Him in an upstairs room having supper. I'm afraid it wasn't an enjoyable meal at all. He had just told them that the time had come for Him to die, and of course they all felt sad and worried. But Jesus wanted so much to comfort His friends that night, and He wanted to tell them more truth about who He was.

To the King that rules forever, who will never die, who cannot be seen, the only God, be honor and glory forever and ever. Amen.

1 TIMOTHY 1:17

7

He said:

"I am the way, and the truth, and the life. The only way to the Father is through me. If you really knew me, you would know my Father, too. But now you do know him, and you have seen him" (John 14:6-7).

Philip felt even more troubled and confused. I'll bet he frowned and puffed with his lips and wrinkled his forehead. What was Jesus saying? It didn't make sense to him. When had he ever seen God the Father? He just had to know what this meant. So he blurted out the thought in his heart.

Philip said to him, "Lord, show us the Father. That is all we need" (John 14:8).

Jesus must have looked right into Philip's eyes. His voice must have been soft, and maybe a little sad. Maybe He reached out and put His hand on Philip's shoulder.

Jesus answered, "I have been with you a long time now. Do you still not know me, Philip? Whoever has seen me has seen the Father. So why do you say, 'Show us the Father'? Don't you believe that I am in the Father and the Father is in me?" (John 14:9-10)

Oh, Philip. Don't you understand yet? Oh, My dear friend, don't you see?

Jesus, the Son of God, was all anyone needed to see of God. The more we learn about Jesus, the more we learn about God. The more we come to know and love Jesus, the more we know and love God.

I don't know if I understand all these things very well myself, but this is something the Bible tells us again and again, so it must be very important. God's Word says:

9

No one can see God, but Jesus Christ is exactly like him (Colossians 1:15).

No one has ever seen God. But God the only Son is very close to the Father, and he has shown us what God is like (John 1:18).

The Son reflects the glory of God and shows us exactly what he is like (Hebrews 1:3).

God the Father looks like Jesus. And Jesus looks like God the Father.

That's very good to know, but there's something else that's even more surprising to me. The more you and I love and obey Jesus, the more *we* begin to look like Him! I'm not kidding.

Paul wrote these words:

We all show the Lord's glory, and we are being changed to be like him. This change in us brings ever greater glory, which comes from the Lord (2 Corinthians 3:18).

When men or women have loved and obeyed Jesus for a long time, there is something about them that people notice. They look like themselves, of course, but sometimes…just for a moment or two…they look like Someone Else. They sound like themselves, too, but sometimes…in the middle of conversation…they sound like Someone Else.

Somehow, they remind people of God.

Somehow, they remind people of Jesus.

I think that's the way it was with Mrs. Eickmeyer.

Maybe God didn't look very much like her but…to me, she looked a lot like God.

Yes, dear friends, we are already God's children. We can't imagine what it is going to be like later on. But we do know that when he comes we will be like him.

1 JOHN 3:2, SLB

10

HOW COULD THERE BE A GOD SO BIG?

The more we think about how BIG God is, the more our poor heads feel dizzy. How could anyone be so great? How could anyone be so strong? How could anyone be so wise? How could…how could…how could…(well, you see what I mean).

Many people in the world for many years have worshiped lots of *little* gods. (Of course we know they are made-up gods, because there is no God but God!)

These little pretend gods are very different from our Heavenly Father.

They can't do everything our God can.

They don't know everything our God knows.

They aren't pure and holy like our God is.

They don't love people the way our God loves.

They don't rule fairly the way our God rules.

Why would people worship puny little gods like these?

I wonder.

Do you think they might be afraid of how bright and powerful and good our God really is? Do you think they want a god who's small enough to understand? Small enough to argue with? Small enough to hide from? Small enough to shut out of their heart and thoughts?

When you think about it, a little god doesn't make much sense.

It took a big God to make everything you see out your window.

It took a big God to make big oceans, big mountains, big rivers, and big heat-shimmery deserts.

It took a big God to make stars beyond counting and worlds beyond imagining.

It took a big, wise God to make all of the tiny things, too. Perfect snowflakes, no two alike. Flowers so small you have to lie on your stomach to look at them. Bright tiny fish—little darts of color—that play tag in a hundred oceans. Pebble-sized diamonds that grab a sunbeam and toss it back as a rainbow. The tiny parts of our bodies that keep us alive and allow us to see and breathe and hug and taste and remember and run and sing praise to our Lord.

I really don't know how God could be so big. But I know that to do all He's done and be all He is, He *has* to be big.

Sometimes when we don't know how to understand or explain something about God, one of the best things we can do is just start praising Him for what we *do* understand. That's what Jeremiah did, and he wrote these words:

Oh, Lord GOD, you made the skies and the earth with your very great power. There is nothing too hard for you to do. You show love and kindness to thousands of people…Great and powerful God, your name is the LORD All-Powerful. You plan and do great things (Jeremiah 32:17, 18, 19).

What can you praise God for today?

I can promise you something right now…He's not too big to bend down and listen to every word!

DOES GOD THINK MUCH ABOUT ME?

*I*t was the middle of the afternoon, and Nathanael was resting under a fig tree. Now, if you lived where Nathanael did, you would understand why he was under a tree instead of running around doing this and that.

Nathanael lived in Israel, and the afternoons could be so hot. Unless you live in Arizona, you can't imagine how hot it got. There weren't any fans or air conditioners in those days (or sprinklers to run through, either), so one of the best places you could be was in the cool shade of some big, leafy tree.

I'm not sure exactly what Nathanael was doing under the tree that afternoon.

But I have an idea.

I think he *might* have been leaning back against the twisty old trunk, looking off into the endless blue of the summer sky…watching the shapes of clouds…and wondering in his heart if God really cared about him very much.

The Bible tells us that Nathanael was a good and honest man, but even good, honest people get a tad discouraged now and then. Maybe he was feeling unhappy about some things that were happening (or *weren't* happening) in his life in those days. Maybe, in the back of his mind, he was beginning to wonder if God really thought about him…if God really loved him.

I can almost hear him whisper under the leaves of that tree.

Lord, do You think about me very much?

Do You care about what happens to me very much?

Do Your thoughts ever come near ol' Nathanael, sitting under a tree, or are You too busy moving stars around and running the world and doing so many important things?

If You really DO love me and think about me...I just wish...somehow...(I know this is silly)...You would let me know.

Just about that time, Nathanael's friend Philip came puffing down the road, red-faced, in a hurry, looking this way and that. Then he saw Nathanael, resting in the shade. Philip started talking right away, and he seemed antsy and excited about something.

Philip found Nathanael and told him, "We have found the man that Moses wrote about in the law, and the prophets also wrote about him. He is Jesus, the son of Joseph, from Nazareth."

But Nathanael [maybe still feeling a little glum] said to Philip, "Can any good thing come from Nazareth?"

Philip answered, "Come and see."

As Jesus saw Nathanael coming toward him, he said, "Here is truly an Israelite. There is nothing false in him."

Nathanael asked, "How do you know me?"

Jesus answered, "I saw you when you were under the fig tree, before Philip told you about me."

Then Nathanael said to Jesus, "Teacher, you are the Son of God; you are the King of Israel" (John 1:45-49).

Now Nathanael *knew!*

Jesus the Lord was thinking about him under that tree!

God's own Son saw him there and loved him. Nathanael had thought he was alone, but he wasn't! Nathanael had stared at the big empty sky and listened to the wind whisper in the silver-green leaves and thought God didn't care about him. But God did! And now he knew!

Tell me something...does God think about YOU very much?

Does He keep His eye on you through the day and all night long? Does He listen in to your thoughts? Does He take notice every time you laugh, every time you sigh, every time a tear falls from your eye? When you find yourself thinking about Him, is He thinking about *you* at the very same time?

Yes, that's really the way it is with our heavenly Father and our Lord Jesus.

When David finally understood how much God thought about him, he wrote this song:

You saw me before I was born.

You planned each day of my life

> *before I began to breathe.*

Every day was recorded in your book!

How precious this is, Lord!

How great to know you think about me all the time!

I can't even count how many times

> *your thoughts turn toward me.*

And when I wake in the morning,

> *you are still thinking of me!*

(Psalm 139:16-18, SLB)

Nathanael asked, "How do you know me?" Jesus answered, "I saw you when you were under the fig tree, before Philip told you about me."

JOHN 1:48

14

Have you ever called someone on the phone and had him or her say, "I'm glad you called. I was just thinking about you!"

That's what happens every time you close your eyes and say a prayer to God. Whether you hear Him or not, He will always say, "How good to hear your voice! I'm so glad you thought about Me, because *I was just thinking about you.*"

WHY DOESN'T GOD TALK TO ME OUT LOUD?

There are times when all of us wish God would say things right out loud. Sometimes I wish He would say, "I love you"

...when I'm wondering if He really does.

Sometimes I wish He would say, "Take this path"

...when I don't know which way to go.

Sometimes I wish He would say, "I'm right beside you"

...when I'm feeling so all alone.

Sometimes I wish He would say, "Don't do that!"

...when I'm about to get myself into trouble (again!).

Sometimes I wish He would say, "I'll protect you"

...when I'm afraid.

Sometimes I wish He would say, "Go here" or "Do that" or "Pick this one"

...when I can't make up my mind.

Why won't He say those things? Why won't He talk to me?

Of course you know that God does speak to people at times—and even out loud, when He wants to. He spoke to lots of men and women in the Bible. Sometimes He did it in a vision, sometimes He did it in a dream, sometimes He spoke through one of His servants, and sometimes He just said things right out loud, plain as you please.

Do you remember the story about young Samuel? The Lord spoke to him when he was just a little boy. The trouble was, Samuel didn't know who was talking!

Here's what the Bible says:

The boy Samuel served the LORD under Eli. In those days the LORD did not speak directly to people very often; there were very few visions.

Eli's eyes were so weak he was almost blind. One night he was lying in bed. Samuel was also in bed in the LORD's house....

Then the LORD called Samuel, and Samuel answered, "I am here!" He ran to Eli and said, "I am here. You called me."

But Eli said, "I didn't call you. Go back to bed." So Samuel went back to bed (1 Samuel 3:1-5).

This happened three times! Finally Eli, the old, blind priest, understood what was happening.

Then Eli realized the LORD was calling the boy. So he told Samuel, "Go to bed. If he calls you again, say, 'Speak, LORD. I

15

am your servant and I am listening.'" So Samuel went and lay down in bed.

The LORD came and stood there and called as he had before, "Samuel, Samuel!"

Samuel said, "Speak, LORD. I am your servant and I am listening" (1 Samuel 3:8-10).

Wouldn't that be *something*? A little scary maybe, but exciting, too.

The Lord told Samuel some important things that night, right out loud, just like you might talk to your best friend.

Why doesn't He talk to you and me like that?

Samuel grew up to become what the Bible calls a "prophet." God used to talk to people through these special men and women. When you wanted to know what God thought about something, you went to the prophet and *he* talked to God for you.

As the years went by, God's prophets and servants began writing down God's words. A number of years after Jesus died and rose again, *all* of the words God wanted written down had been written down. They were put together in a book we call the Bible. Now we don't have to look for a prophet when we want to hear God. All we have to do is open up our Bible and read! God's Holy Spirit loves to help us understand all those good words.

One man a long time ago got so excited about God's words that he sat down and wrote *176 reasons* why he loved them so much. Later, those reasons became a part of the Bible, too. You can see them all in Psalm 119.

These are the kind of things he wrote:

How can a young person live a pure life?
     By obeying your word. v. 9

Your rules give me pleasure;
     they give me good advice. v. 24

I am sad and tired.
     Make me strong again as you have promised. v. 28

When I suffer, this comforts me:
     Your promise gives me life. v. 50

Your teachings are worth more to me
     than thousands of pieces of gold and silver. v. 72

LORD, your word is everlasting;
     it continues forever in heaven. v. 89

I am wiser than all my teachers,
     because I think about your rules. v. 99

Your promises are sweet to me,
     sweeter than honey in my mouth! v. 103

Your word is like a lamp for my feet
     and a light for my path. v. 105

You are my hiding place and my shield;
     I hope in your word. v. 114

Give me your helping hand,
     because I have chosen your commands. v. 173

Now those were only a *few* of his reasons. If you wanted to ask him *all* his reasons, you'd better get a chair and sit down. It might take a long time!

Your word is like a lamp for my feet and a light for my path.
PSALM 119:105

17

Why did he love God's Word so much?

(Take a deep breath…) Because it kept his life clean. It gave him good advice. It made him strong when he was sad and tired. It made him happy. It gave him comfort. It was better than a whole room piled up with money. It will last forever. It was always with him. It made him wiser than his teachers. It always tasted sweet. It shone on his path like the brightest light. It was a hiding place in trouble and a shield in battle. It was like a strong helping hand.

That man was so excited about God's wonderful Word! Do you think it bothered him much that he never heard God talk out loud? No! He didn't *need* to hear God's voice, because he had God's own words! He had God's good counsel wherever he went.

That's the best part. By reading the Bible, we can hear God whenever we want to! We can listen to Him speak wherever we are, whatever we're doing. And if we have some of His Word memorized—hidden away in our hearts—we don't even need to have a Bible in front of us.

Does God speak in other ways, besides the Bible?

Well, yes, sometimes He whispers things in our hearts and lets us know what He wants us to do. And He may even talk out loud to you someday, like He talked to little Samuel. (It's always good to remember that God can do *whatever* He wants to do, *whenever* He wants to do it, and He doesn't have to explain anything to anybody.)

But even if He never talks out loud to me, I know at least 176 reasons why the Bible is all that I need!

WHY DID GOD MAKE PEOPLE, ANYWAY? WAS HE LONELY?

Those are good questions, but I'd like a turn to ask you a question, too. *Why do people adopt children?* Why do boy-less and girl-less grown-ups want to add mom-less and dad-less boys and girls to their families?

Is it just because they are lonely and need some company? Are their houses so still and quiet they need the sound of giggles and squeals and bumps and bangs and little feet running up and down the stairs?

Maybe. But I think people who adopt little boys and girls are people with some extra things in their lives. I don't mean extra room in their home or extra money in the bank, or extra time in their day. I mean extra things in their *hearts*.

I think they have extra love…and wonder who could use some.

I think they have extra patience…and wonder who they could lend it to.

I think they have extra wisdom about life…and wonder who might need a little.

I think they have extra kindness…and wonder who might especially like to have some.

I think they have extra gentleness…and wonder who might have been missing some for a long, long time.

Do you suppose that's the way it was with God? Maybe He said something to Himself like this: "I am happy and peaceful

and patient and wise. I am full of love. I *am* love. I would like to give some of Myself away."

So do you know what He did?

First, He made angels. That was the first part of His plan—and once He got started, you just can't believe how many angels He made. It probably takes someone as wise as God just to keep count of them all. When God created angels, He shared some of His light and beauty and holiness. He gave them some of His strength and wisdom and joy. And the angels came to life—millions and millions of them—like new stars winking in a great night sky. How those fresh-made angels shone! Can't you just see them trying out their new wings and blazing across the heavens like shooting stars? (Now, I'm not sure at all that angels have wings, since I've never seen one. But somehow, it seems like they *ought* to.)

Did God give too much of Himself away when He made angels? Was there any *less* of Him after He was done? Not a bit! Did He have any love and wisdom and strength left over? Oh yes—He had as much as He ever did. God can never be any less than He always is.

So then God made the heavens and the earth. That was the next part of His plan. He filled our world with mountains and valleys and rivers. He planted the world with trees and grass and bushes and flowers and fruit and vegetables (yes, even broccoli). He made animals and birds and fish to play in the sun-dappled meadows and soar in the clean, blue skies and leap in the laughing seas.

Do you know what came next in God's great plan? He made people to put on this beautiful world!

He made a man and a woman and He made them so they could have children (God thinks of everything, doesn't He?). God knew that soon there would be the sound of giggles and squeals and bumps and bangs and little feet tearing up and down the pathways of a brand new world.

And God had so much love and wisdom and joy to share with His people.

But we know what happened don't we? On one sad day—maybe the saddest day that ever was—the people God made turned away from Him and stopped loving Him.

What happened then? Was God out of love and kindness? Was He out of faithfulness and patience? (I'm sure I would have been.)

No. He had more love to share. He had more of Himself to give.

More than even the wisest angels could have imagined.

He had so much love He gave His own precious Son to die for these people who had stopped loving Him.

And now, for all who receive His Son Jesus as their Savior from sin (even you and me!), He offers them a Forever Home in Heaven. He offers them His love and all that He has and all that He is…forever.

Who could have ever believed God would have so much to give?

I don't know about you, but it makes me want to love Him back with all my heart. It makes me want to sing the best songs of praise and thanks to Him that I know—and maybe even make up a few new ones.

Would God have been lonely for me if He'd never created me? Would God have been lonely for you if He'd never created you?

Well—I guess we don't have to wonder about that, because He DID create a me and He DID create a you. It was His good plan all along.

I'm so very glad He had enough *extra* love to let me and you into His big, happy family.

CAN I HIDE FROM GOD?

When I was a boy, I had a friend named Steve who liked to dig holes. One Saturday morning he borrowed his dad's shovel and dug the biggest, deepest hole he'd ever dug.

He shoveled all day in the soft dirt of a field behind his house. Then, when the hole was just the way he wanted it, he covered the top with a wide sheet of plywood. (I wouldn't try this if I were you—you never know when a hole might cave in on your head!)

Steve called that covered-up hole his "underground fort" and kept a lot of his best treasures down there...some of his favorite rocks and marbles and a dart gun and little green army men and a couple really good comic books—that kind of stuff.

To get into his fort, he would slide the plywood back a little and slither down inside the hole. Then he would slide the board back, turn on his red and silver Cub Scout flashlight, and there he was! He didn't feel like a little boy in a dark hole at all; he felt more like a powerful warrior in a great fortress.

(He let me down inside it once, and it smelled muddy and rooty and didn't seem at all like a great fortress to me.)

The thing is, no one could *see* Steve in his underground fort.

His friends couldn't see him. His brothers and sisters couldn't see him. His mom and dad couldn't see him. His dog Cleo couldn't see him either, but I think she knew where he was, because she kept snuffling and woofing all around the edges of the plywood.

Steve really liked the idea that no one knew where he was— and he liked to brag about it, too. Do you know what he told me once?

He bragged that not even *God* could see him in his fort.

He thought he could do whatever he wanted to do in that hole and no one would know. He really thought he had somehow disappeared from God's sight.

Well, I knew Steve was wrong about that, and I told him so, too. But he just laughed. A long time later I learned what the Bible says about hiding from God. (I wish I had known those things when I was arguing with Steve!) Listen to what David wrote:

I can never be lost to your Spirit!

   I can never get away from my God!

...I might try to hide in the darkness.

   But the night becomes light around me.

For even the darkness cannot hide from God.

   To you the night shines as bright as day

   (Psalm 139:7, 11-12, SLB).

21

At another time, the Lord told His servant Jeremiah that people who disobeyed God could not hide from Him. They couldn't hide in the hills and mountains. They couldn't hide in caves or big cracks in the rocks. *"I see everything they do…,"* the Lord said. *"Am I a God who is only in one place? Do they think I cannot see what they are doing? Can anyone hide from me? Am I not everywhere in Heaven and earth at the same time?"* *(Jeremiah 16:17; 23:24, SLB).*

God didn't have any problem at all looking through that muddy plywood at the little boy underneath. His eyes can see through anything. He can see into underground forts. He can see into basements and closets and bedrooms—and even under the bed. He can see through thick stone walls.

He sees astronauts floating in their space shuttles and knows what they are thinking. He sees sailors sleeping in their bunks in submarines deep in the ocean and knows what they are dreaming. He sees miners working like ants in dark tunnels, miles under the ground, and hears the tunes they hum to themselves. He sees explorers creeping into black caves under the roots of a great mountain and counts their goose bumps when they get cold. He sees the good things good men and women do in the light and the evil things evil men and women do in the dark.

Even though all this is true, there have always been people who have tried to hide from God.

The very first man and woman, Adam and Eve, tried to hide from God after they disobeyed Him back in the Garden of Eden. Here's what the Bible says:

Then they heard the LORD God walking in the garden during the cool part of the day, and the man and his wife hid from the LORD God among the trees in the garden. But the LORD God called to the man and said, "Where are you?"

The man answered, "I heard you walking in the garden, and I was afraid…so I hid" (Genesis 3:8-10).

Do you think God really didn't know where Adam and Eve were? Do you think they fooled Him by hiding *in the trees?* No, I don't think so, either.

I think when God said, "Where are you?" His voice was very sad. I think He meant, *"Why are you hiding from Me, Adam? What happened? Why didn't you come and meet Me? Why aren't you here to go walking with Me as we always do? Why has your heart changed?"*

Jonah tried to hide from God, too. When God asked him to go to a certain city and warn the people there, Jonah said "No way" and ran in the other direction! (Can you imagine that?)

He went to the city of Joppa, where he found a ship that was going to the city of Tarshish. Jonah paid for the trip and went aboard, planning to go to Tarshish to run away from the LORD…

Jonah had gone down far inside the ship to lie down, and he fell fast asleep (Jonah 1:3, 5).

I guess Jonah thought he could give God the slip by sailing away to a far city. I guess he thought he could hide from God's eyes by climbing down the ladder in the ship and curling up in a dark corner behind some barrels and boxes.

But God knew right where he was. And He knew that His disobedient servant was in for a couple of unpleasant surprises. (Do you know what those surprises were?)

I might try to hide in the darkness. But the night becomes light around me. For even the darkness cannot hide from God. To you the night shines as bright as day.

PSALM 139:11-12

23

You can't hide from God in an underground fort.

You can't hide from God in the trees.

You can't hide from God in a ship out in the ocean.

God knows where you are all the time. He's never lost sight of you for a moment.

Maybe the real question is, why would anyone *want* to hide from God? Why would we want to hide from Someone who loves us so much? Is it because we know we've disobeyed Him? Then let's hurry back to Him and tell Him we're sorry! How silly to hide in bushes or boxes or dark, muddy holes when we could be in the light and walk and talk with our wonderful God!

JUST HOW MUCH DOES GOD LOVE ME?

*M*any truths about God are TOO BIG for our minds to hold. We can know some of the truth—and it shines in our hands like star-bright jewels. But there is always more and more and *more*. More than we can ever know.

We can know a little about God's love, but we could never begin to reach our thoughts around something so mighty.

Sometimes it helps me to think about it like this…

Imagine God's love is a huge castle, soaring higher than a thousand white-peaked mountains—linked together—with their tops poking into space. Imagine looking at this castle from far away. There it is…vast and high, gleaming like morning sun on new snow. Its towers reach up and up toward Heaven. Its windows blaze with bright, welcome light.

This castle is *so great* it would take a lifetime just to walk around it.

You'd love to find out everything you could about that beautiful castle. And there is so much to see and taste and know. Its gardens are bigger than your whole state (even if you live in Alaska) and spill over with towering trees and flowering trees and leaping fountains and majestic waterfalls and deep, bubbling springs and a rainbow of singing birds and—well, who knows what else. Its rooms are filled up with wondrous treasures and music and laughter and mysteries and places where you can explore and play and hide and rest.

No one has seen all its rooms and towers.

No one has eaten in all its long, sunny banquet halls.

No one has peered through all its high windows.

But do you know what?

That castle can be *mine*, because God loves me.

And the castle can be *yours*, because God loves you.

When does it become yours? Just like any other gift, it becomes yours when you *receive* it.

And God wants you to come near that castle and see how dazzling and grand it is. He wants you to walk in through its wide

doorway and fill your eyes and ears and hands with all its wonders and delights—until the light and love fill you all the way up and you can't hold any more in your heart or your pockets.

Can you know all of it? No. Not in this world. Not even in a trillion years in Heaven.

But you can find a special room in that castle. A room you'll love so very much. And you can get to know that room, look out of your own window, and at the end of the day curl up in a big soft chair and fall asleep.

Every bit of the castle belongs to you and me, but small as we humans are, we can only enjoy and understand just so much at a time. But we have the rest of our lives here on Earth and endless life in Heaven to keep learning and seeing and hearing more and more.

This is the castle of God's love.

But there are other castles, too!

Castles of His endless wisdom.

Castles of His mighty strength.

Castles of His shining goodness.

And so many more.

With so MUCH to see and know…let's not be in too big a hurry, okay? Let's learn a *little* more about God and find some places in His love and wisdom that feel just like home.

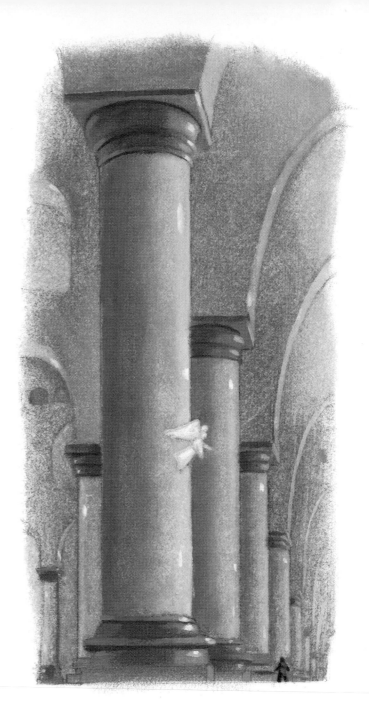

WHERE WAS JESUS BEFORE HE WAS BORN?

We know that Jesus is God, just as God the Father is God. So He must have been somewhere *before* He was born on Earth.

Of course we all like to think about Him being born on a dark Christmas night, so long ago. The best and greatest night that ever was. It was such an amazing night that people from South America to Iceland take time every year to remember it. People from Greenslide, British Columbia, to Redrock, Texas, give gifts and drink egg nog and light candles and hum Christmas carols—even if they don't really understand what it's all about. (But *you* do, don't you?)

Jesus, the Son of God, came into the world as a newborn baby, just as so many of God's servants and friends for hundreds of years said He would. Can you remember some of those promises, given to people those many long years before that first Christmas night?

A child has been born to us; God has given a son to us.

He will be responsible for leading his people.

His name will be Wonderful Counselor, Powerful God,

Father Who Lives Forever, Prince of Peace.

Power and peace will be in his kingdom

and will continue to grow forever

(Isaiah 9:6).

Yes, the prophets said this wonder would come into the world, this boy-child would be born in Bethlehem, and this old Earth would never, never be the same. And the most surprising truth of all is that this baby was God's own Son!

Before He became a baby on Earth, Jesus had lived in Heaven with God the Father, God the Holy Spirit, and all the millions of shining, busy angels. This is what His friend John wrote about Him:

Before anything else existed, there was God's Son. He was the Word, and he was with God. He has always been alive and is himself God. He created everything there is. Nothing exists that he didn't make. Eternal life is in him. This life gives light to all mankind…And Christ became a human being and lived on earth among us. He was full of loving forgiveness and truth. And some of us have seen his glory. He has the glory of the only Son of the Father! (John 1:1-4, 14, SLB).

There came a time—at the best time, the right time—when the mighty Son of God turned His back on all the beauty and happiness of His forever home. And somehow—no one knows just how—He stepped out of Heaven and entered Earth as a baby. Here is what the Bible says about that great, great miracle:

But when the right time came, God sent his Son who was born of a woman (Galatians 4:4).

God's children are human beings, made of flesh and blood. [Jesus] became flesh and blood too by being born in human form (Hebrews 2:14, SLB).

It must have seemed a long way between Heaven and Earth.

It must have been sad to leave such a glorious home.

It must have made the angels wide-eyed and solemn to see the

Before anything else existed, there was God's Son. He was the Word, and he was with God. He has always been alive and is himself God.

JOHN 1:1,2

27

King they love and serve say good-bye and take that long step over the edge of Heaven—

—down

—down

—down

through black space to the little blue-and-brown planet where you and I live. Did the angels know that the man Jesus would have to die? Did they know that when He grew up His strong, gentle hands would be nailed to a cross of wood? Did they know their King would give up His life for all the wrong, hateful things you and I have done?

Did they know those things? I think they probably did.

But it wasn't very long before *they* got to come to Earth, too. Late on a sleepy, star-sprinkled night, those angels peeled back the sky just like you would tear open a sparkling Christmas present. Then, with light and joy pouring out of Heaven like water through a broken dam, they began to shout and sing the message that baby Jesus had been born.

The world had a Savior! The angels called it "Good News," and it was.

·It still is…and I'll bet it always will be.

WHAT DO GOD AND JESUS DO ALL DAY?

God is doing *so many things* all across His wide universe, I couldn't begin to tell it all—even if I knew! Tell me…

What was the sunrise like outside your window this morning? Did you notice…or were you too busy eating your cereal and getting ready for school? (Or maybe you were still in bed with the covers over your sleepy head!)

What was the sunset like last evening? Was it purple and deep red, with touches of pink—edged in soft gold? Did you notice…or were you too busy playing with your friends or eating your dinner?

Did you happen to think about how God was painting those colors across the sky, using just the colors and brushstrokes He wanted to use? Did you happen to remember that no sunrise or sunset you will see in your whole life will ever be just the same as another? God is such a marvelous Artist He never uses exactly the same brush or colors twice.

Now, what ELSE is He doing while He's painting your sunset?

Well…on the *other* side of the world, He's creating a brand new sunrise for boys and girls just getting up over there. And every moment of the day, as the Earth turns and whirls through space, sunrises and sunsets roll across our world in a never-ending, mega-million-colored wave.

And no two of them are ever, *ever* the same.

That's amazing enough to think about by itself. But our world is only ONE little world! How many worlds are out there in deep space, scattered like grains of sand on the Creator's starry shore? No one knows how many worlds.

No one knows how many flaming suns—

blue and white and yellow and red—

coming up and going down—

over so many strange and wonderful places—

where no one has ever walked—

but God.

Sunrises and sunsets everywhere across the universe! Every second. All different. On and on and on.

Sunrises over the fiery hills of Mercury,

sunrises over the rocky red deserts of Mars,

sunrises over the glowing valleys of Venus.

Sunsets over boiling purple seas,

sunsets over towering green mountains of ice,

sunsets over crystal canyons and orange rivers

of molten stone.

You would think all God had time to do was paint, paint, paint. But that's really such a small part of His day—only the thinnest sliver of His greatness. (Maybe painting is what He does for fun, or to make a few serious angels smile. What do you think?)

What ELSE does the Bible say about God's day?

Well, first of all, there really is no "day" or "night" for God. It never gets dark in Heaven, and God never sleeps. He stays awake all the time, and part of what He does when He's awake is watch over you!

My help comes from the LORD…

He will never let me stumble, slip, or fall.

For he is always watching, never sleeping.

The Lord Himself is caring for you!

He is your helper and defender.

He protects you day and night

(Psalm 121:2, 3-7, 8, SLB).

What ELSE does God do with His day?

Did you know that one of the things Jesus does all day is to hold everything together? That's really true. In some mysterious way, the power of God's Son is the "glue" that keeps all Creation from falling apart like a crumbled cracker. The Bible says:

Christ created everything in Heaven and earth. He created the things we can see and the things we can't see…He made them for his own use and glory. He was before all else began. His power holds everything together (Colossians 1:16-17, SLB).

His power keeps the sun shining hot and bright as it climbs its way up the sky.

His power moves the sea and keeps its waves from swallowing up the land.

His power pushes the wind that fills the sails of boats and turns

Christ created everything in Heaven and earth. He created the things we can see and the things we can't see…

COLOSSIANS 1:16-17

31

windmills on the farm and tickles your hair and ripples through the green leaves on lazy summer days.

His power keeps your own body together—blood in your veins, strength in your bones, toes on your feet, fingers on your hands, and a smile on your face. (I guess that last part is up to you!)

Do you know what ELSE He's doing while He's painting the sky, holding everything together, and watching so carefully over you?

The Bible says He is holding out His arms…waiting to save and forgive people who don't know Him, don't love Him, and won't obey Him. God says,

"Here am I, here am I." All day long I have held out my hands to an obstinate [stubborn] people, who walk in ways not good (Isaiah 65:1-2, NIV).

Do you remember the story Jesus told about the boy who ran away from his family, wasted all his money, then ended up poor and lonely and hungry? Do you remember what the story said about that boy's dad? He watched that winding road every day, didn't he? He shaded his eyes and squinted into the sun and looked as far as he could into the hazy distance. He was waiting and waiting and waiting for his boy to come home.

When that boy finally did come stumbling down that long road home, all ragged and dirty and skinny and sad, that dad saw him far away. And then—with tears spilling down his face—the father started running down that road as hard as he could. He grabbed that disobedient, runaway boy of his and laughed and cried and hugged him and kissed him again and again.

Jesus tells us that God is like that dad.

God waits and waits for men and women and boys and girls to turn around from going their own way and run back to Him. When we do, His arms are wide open and there is a smile of welcome and joy on His face. God loves us so much!

What ELSE does God do all day? (While He's painting the sky, holding everything together, watching over you, and holding His arms open wide?)

Well, the next time you're talking to Him, you might just ask Him and see what He says.

Remember, He's never too busy for you!

WHY DOES GOD LET BAD THINGS HAPPEN?

Bad things just keep on happening in our world, don't they? You hear people talking about it and you see them shake their heads.

You see it on TV when your mom and dad watch the news.

Bad stuff. Sad stuff. Things-that-make-you-mad stuff.

Sometimes little babies die.

Sometimes children get very sick.

Sometimes moms and dads can't get along.

Sometimes countries go to war.

32

Sometimes people are hurt in car wrecks.

Sometimes churches and schools are torn up by big storms.

Sometimes farmers' crops are ruined by floods or bugs or hot weather.

We know that God is a good God…so why do awful things like these happen?

Some people (who should know better) say it's because God isn't wise enough or strong enough to *keep* these things from happening. But that's not true, is it? God is the wisest and strongest Person of all. He knows everything and can do anything.

So why do these things happen?

Let me ask *you* something first….

What does it mean when you feel chills running up and down your back? What does it mean when you feel too weak and achey to get out of bed? What does it mean when your throat hurts…and your head aches…and your stomach turns upside down…and your mom says you have a fever?

What do those things mean?

Yes, they might mean you get to stay home from school. But why?

Because you're *sick*, that's why.

Because there is some stubborn, invisible germ attacking your body. That's why you feel the way you do. That's why you can't go outside and ride your bike or go roller-blading or shoot baskets.

Now way back at the beginning of time, something like that came into our world. It wasn't a germ or a virus; it was worse. I can't even tell you how much worse. It made our whole world sick, and do you know what? It's been sick ever since.

What was this terrible thing? What was this disease? It was called "sin."

And it wasn't God who brought sin into our beautiful world; it was the very first man and woman. They *let* sin come in! When Adam and Eve listened to what the serpent said (who was really the devil), they chose in their hearts to disobey God and turn away from His love and protection. When they did that, sin crept into the world and the world changed.

Bad, sad things began to happen right away to Adam and Eve and their family—and those things are still happening to families today. All that is broken won't be fixed and all that is hurt won't be healed until Jesus comes back and becomes King of the whole Earth. (I get excited thinking about KING JESUS, don't you?)

Whenever you see bad things happening in our world

in our country

in your city

in your school

in your neighborhood

in your home

in your own heart

that only shows that sin keeps working its hurt and harm, over and over.

The Bible says:

All people are the same: All have sinned and are not good enough for God's glory (Romans 3:22-23).

Yes, we still have a wonderful, beautiful world, and it is still God's good creation. But underneath the beauty, in the middle of all the greatness and wonder...there is a long, sad sickness in the world that won't go away.

That's why...sometimes...the wind blows too hard, the sun shines too hot, the earth shakes too hard, the snow piles up too high, the rivers overflow with too much water, and animals try to kill and eat each other.

That's why

> ...spiders bite
>
> ...and bees sting
>
> ...and lightning strikes
>
> ...and water drowns
>
> ...and storms blast
>
> ...and sunlight burns
>
> ...and cold chills our bones.

That's why our human bodies don't always work the way we want them to. That's why hearts quit pumping, and legs quit walking, and ears quit hearing, and eyes quit seeing, and minds quit thinking.

34

Now listen carefully. This *doesn't* mean that you—or anyone—gets sick or injured because you have "done something bad." It just means that EVERYONE—good people and bad people, people who love God and people who don't—has to live with bodies that are sometimes weak and must someday die.

Our human hearts are sick with the sin disease, too. That's why soldiers shoot at each other. That's why men and women fight each other, hurt each other, lie to each other, steal from each other, and say terrible things to each other.

Now this is all very sad and not much fun to think about. But don't quit reading now, because this story has a happy ending!

Jesus was the only person ever born who was NOT sick with sin. There was NO sin-germ in His heart when He was born. He NEVER sinned through all the days of His life. He was the ONLY person who could ever take away all the sin-sickness of the whole world.

And He did it!

When He died on the cross, He took *all* of that horrible sickness and darkness into Himself. The Bible says,

For God took the sinless Christ and poured into him our sins (2 Corinthians 5:21, SLB).

Christ carried our sins in his body on the cross so we would stop living for sin and start living for what is right (1 Peter 2:24).

Those who gladly receive the Lord Jesus as their Savior have their sins forgiven! They get to start life again with fresh, new hearts. They have God's wonderful Holy Spirit to help them through all the troubles and hurts of life. And when they die, they get to live with God in His perfect Heaven forever!

Until then...until that good day when we walk through Heaven's bright front door and say hello to everyone waiting to see us...until then...you and I and everyone we love have to

live in a world badly hurt by sin. Bad things will keep on happening until King Jesus comes back with all His mighty angels to set things right again.

And He will.

But until He does, God will love us and help us and comfort us and sometimes heal us. He will give us so many GOOD THINGS that our hearts will be filled up with gladness and hope. The GOOD THINGS God gives us will help us get through the sad times and the bad times. And we can help other people with *their* bad times and tell them about a good God who loves them so very much.

When we do, King Jesus is very pleased.

WHY DIDN'T JESUS STAY ON EARTH?

When Jesus died on the cross, His friends couldn't have felt much worse. It was more horrible than losing your dad, your brother, your favorite teacher, and your best buddy all at the same time.

But then…He came out of that grave *alive* again! Alive forever! This made the Lord's followers so wildly happy they hardly knew which way was up.

But then…just a few weeks after that, He went back to Heaven and left them *again*.

Don't you think they must have been…well, disappointed?

It must have been like having someone you really love drive up in the driveway, come into the house and hug everybody, then get right back in the car and zoom away again. It would leave you feeling kind of empty. You'd feel kind of like your dog feels when he trots into the warm house through the front door and then gets put right back out through the back door!

Why didn't Jesus stay?

Why did He have to leave?

Why did He have to go back to His Father's house?

Why can't He be here *right now*?

Why can't we go for walks, or skip rocks across the river, or play Monopoly, or just sit close together and talk sometimes? Wouldn't that be *great*? But that's not going to happen, is it? Because Jesus is going to stay in Heaven until the time comes for Him to come back to Earth again as the great King of Kings.

Now of course it's a wonderful thing to think about—Jesus coming back on a big white horse, wearing a crown, carrying a bright, sharp sword, and making the world right again. But it still means that He's *not here yet* and…well, maybe we wish sometimes that He were.

Our Lord's disciples felt the same way when He told them He was about to leave.

Jesus said, "My children, I will be with you only a little longer. You will look for me, and what I told the Jews, I tell you now: Where I am going you cannot come…."

Simon Peter asked Jesus, "Lord, where are you going?"

Jesus answered, "Where I am going you cannot follow now, but you will follow later."

Peter asked, "Lord why can't I follow now?" (John 13:33, 36-37)

How did Jesus comfort His friends? What did He say to help them?

First, He said He was going to get a place ready for them in His Father's house. And then He was going to come back and get them, and they would be with Him always.

That might have made them feel a little better. But then He said something more. Something amazing.

"I will ask the Father, and he will send you another Helper to be with you forever—the Spirit of truth. The world cannot accept him, because it does not see him or know him. But you know him, because he lives with you and he will be in you" *(John 14:16-17).*

Another Helper? To be with us always? Who is that?

Jesus explained:

"The Helper will teach you everything and will cause you to remember all that I told you. This Helper is the Holy Spirit whom the Father will send in my name.... Your hearts are filled with sadness because I have told you these things. But I tell you the truth, it is better for you that I go away. When I go away, I will send the Helper to you. If I do not go away, the Helper will not come" (14:26; 16:6-7).

Better? It was BETTER that Jesus went away? How could it be better? Why is it better to have the Helper, the Holy Spirit with us?

I can think of one reason. (I know there must be lots more.)

When Jesus was on Earth in His human body, He could only be in one place at one time. But the Holy Spirit can be everywhere at once! He can be with me out on my mountain bike at the same time He's with you by the fireplace in your living room. He can be helping me with a worry at the same time He's teaching you more about Jesus. He can be talking gently to me about something wrong in my life at the same time He's cheering you up with a verse from the Bible.

Do you remember the story about the two followers of Jesus who were walking along the road after Jesus had died and had risen from the dead?

You know how it is when you *really* get talking to someone else about something and you get so interested that you hardly know where you are. Well as these two people were hiking along and gabbing a-mile-a-minute and interrupting each other and waving their arms around, Someone walked up beside them. It was Jesus! But somehow, they didn't recognize Him. He spoke to His friends:

"What are these things you are talking about while you walk?"

The two followers stopped, looking very sad. The one named Cleopas answered, "Are you the only visitor in Jerusalem who does not know what just happened there?"

Jesus said to them, "What are you talking about?"

They said, "About Jesus of Nazareth…" (Luke 24:17-19).

They told this Stranger about everything that had happened. How Jesus had died on a cross and was buried. They told Him about the empty grave and the stories that Jesus had come back to life. And then, while they walked along that dusty, gravelly road, Jesus took time to explain many things to them. He helped them understand what the Bible said about God's Son dying for our sins.

Later that night, as they sat down to dinner together, Jesus said the blessing, started to hand them some food—then—in the blink of an eye—He disappeared! They knew who it was *then*, but He was gone! Didn't even stay for dessert.

It was wonderful for Cleopas and his friend when Jesus was there with them, explaining the Bible to them and encouraging them to believe in God. But while He was on the road with those two…who was explaining things to poor old Peter? Who was urging John not to be sad? Who was teaching Thomas not to doubt? Who was helping Mary and Martha to be strong? Who was reminding Philip of what Jesus had said?

The Holy Spirit can do all those things at once! He is God, just as the Father is God and Jesus is God. And Jesus said that He comes to live *inside* the hearts of those who love God. That's why He's called THE HELPER.

He's always there with us.

He's always there to help us.

He's always there to comfort us.

He's always there to encourage us.

He's always there to teach us.

He's always there to show us the best way.

He's always there to remind us about Jesus.

He will be with us FOREVER.

Someday, maybe not too long from this day (you never know), we will all be in Heaven together with our Heavenly Father, the Lord Jesus, the Holy Spirit, and so many beautiful angels it will make your head spin. But until that time, while we're still on this old Earth, we have the Holy Spirit to be our special Helper, Partner, Friend, and Teacher.

Jesus said that would be the best thing for you and me.

And if *Jesus* said it's best, then you can know

it is certainly

without a doubt

the very, very BEST!

WHEN WILL JESUS COME BACK?

The Bible says Jesus is not only coming back, He's coming back *twice*. Now sometimes I do things twice because I don't do it right the first time. But Jesus does things right every time.

So why would He come back to Earth at two different times?

Probably because He's coming back for two different reasons!

The first time He comes back, He is coming to keep His promise to His church—all the people who love and obey Him. Remember what He said to His men on that last night they were together?

"Don't let your hearts be troubled. Trust in God, and trust in me. There are many rooms in my Father's house. I would not tell you this if it were not true. I am going there to prepare a

place for you. After I go and prepare a place for you, I will come back and take you to be with me so that you may be where I am" (John 14:1-3).

When Jesus lived on earth, He was a carpenter and built good things with wood. When Jesus went back to Heaven, He kept right on building things—much better things! He told His followers that He would be getting a place ready for them (and for us, too!) when they finally came home to Heaven. Now I can't tell you if He's been building with wood or gold or jewels or the light from a sunrise—or something grander and finer than we can even imagine. But I do know He's been busy at it because He said so.

When He comes back the first time, He won't come all the way down to Earth. He will come just as far as the clouds and then call us UP from there. Isn't that exciting to think about? Just listen!

Some of us will be living when the Lord comes back. But we won't rise to meet him before those who are in their graves. The Lord himself will come down from heaven. This will happen with a mighty shout. There will be the voice of the archangel and a trumpet of God. The believers who are dead will be the first to rise to meet the Lord. Then we who are alive will be caught up with them. We will go to the clouds to meet the Lord in the air. We will stay with him forever. (1 Thessalonians 4:15-17, SLB).

Wow! What a moment that will be!

There you are in school on a lazy afternoon, sneaking a look out the window for a moment—and suddenly you hear the clear, silver blast of a trumpet and a shout that shakes like thunder.

Then—before you know it—you're up out of your chair.

Before you can blink, you're up out of your classroom.

We will go to the clouds to meet the Lord in the air. We will stay with him forever.
1 THESSALONIANS
4:17

40

Before you can gasp, you're high over the school, flying in the air like a missile, and up, up, up toward the clouds.

And what do you see in those clouds? You see Jesus, waiting to welcome you. You see a sky full of excited angels, flying around, watching it all, and doing whatever angels are supposed to do. You see all your family and friends who love Jesus. You even see people who have died and have been in Heaven for a long time. And everyone is laughing and shouting and crying for joy and praising God and maybe even doing backflips on top of the clouds. (I think I'd like to try that once or twice.)

Then on you go with that whole happy crowd of millions…higher and higher and HIGHER until Heaven's gate swings wide open to let everyone in. The bright happiness and music and laughter that greets you there will go on forever and ever.

But why will Jesus only come as far as the clouds that first time?

Because the *next* time He puts His foot down on the Earth, He will be coming as the King of Kings. He will be coming to destroy His enemies and judge all the hurtful, evil things in the world and to make things right again.

Listen to what it will be like when He comes back for the last time:

Then I saw Heaven opened and a white horse standing there. The one sitting on the horse was named Faithful and True. He is the one who justly punishes and makes war. His eyes were like flames, and on his head were many crowns. A name was written on his forehead, and only he knew its meaning. He was clothed with garments dipped in blood. His title was "The Word of God." The armies of Heaven followed him on white horses. They were dressed in finest linen, white and clean.

In his mouth he held a sharp sword to strike down the nations. He ruled them with an iron grip…On his robe and thigh was written, "King of kings and Lord of lords" (Revelation 19:11-16, SLB).

When will all this happen?

When will He call me to meet Him in the clouds?

When will He come charging through space on that white horse with the shining armies of Heaven following behind?

The Bible gives us a very simple answer.

SOON.

That's the very word the Lord Jesus used.

"I am coming soon. Continue strong in your faith" (Revelation 3:11).

"Listen! I am coming soon!" (Revelation 22:7).

"Yes, I am coming soon" (Revelation 22:20).

Nobody knows the day (or the night) when Jesus will come back. If they say they know, they're not telling the truth, because Jesus says NO ONE knows.

"No one knows when that day or time will be, not the angels in heaven, not even the Son. Only the Father knows…. So always be ready, because you don't know the day your Lord will come (Matthew 24:36, 42).

All we *need* to know is that Jesus is coming soon, just as He said.

And if He said it was SOON two thousand years ago, think how much *SOONER* it is now!

I want so much to be ready. Don't you?

I want my heart to be right when He comes back for me. You too?

I'll tell you what…if you'll pray for me once in a while, I'll be sure to pray for you! And if I don't see you sooner, I'll look for you on top of that big white cloud, high in the wide blue sky. I think you'll know me…I'll be the one trying to do backflips.

HOW CAN I KNOW FOR SURE I'M GOING TO HEAVEN?

Going to Heaven is so important, you want to be very, very sure that's where you'll be when the time comes to leave this life.

And you *can* be sure. You don't have to wonder. You don't have to be afraid or worry. Jesus came all the way from Heaven to make the way plain and clear. He said:

"I tell you the truth, whoever hears what I say and believes in the One who sent me has eternal life. That person will not be judged guilty but has already left death and has entered life." (John 5:24)

Paul wanted to make the way plain and clear, too. He wrote:

"All people have sinned and are not good enough for God's glory.…When people sin, they earn what sin pays—death. But God gives us a free gift—life forever in Christ Jesus our Lord" (Romans 3:23; 6:23).

John wanted us to understand, too. He wrote these words about Jesus:

"To all who received him, to those who believed in his name, he gave the right to become children of God" (John 1:12, NIV).

When you are ready to give your life to Jesus, you might say a prayer to Him something like this.

Dear Lord Jesus, thank You for inviting me to Your beautiful Forever Home. Thank You for inviting me to be a child of God. Thank You for bleeding and dying on the cross for all the bad, hurtful things I have done. I want to belong to You. I want You to be Lord and King of my life. Please forgive me for the bad things in my heart. I want my life to belong to You right now and forever! Please come into my life and be with me always. Amen.

Did you pray that prayer? Did you understand it? Did you mean it with all your heart? Then watch for me when you come to Heaven someday! And I'll be watching for you, too! Being all together with Jesus will be…AWESOME!

To all who received him, to those who believed in his name, he gave the right to become children of God.

JOHN 1:12